This Little Pig Went to Market

This Little Pig Went to Market

Play Rhymes for Infants and
Young Children
compiled by

NORAH
MONTGOMERIE

Illustrated by Margery Gill

THE BODLEY HEAD
LONDON SYDNEY
TORONTO

To my Mother

ISBN 0 370 01079 5
© Norah Montgomerie 1966
Illustrations © The Bodley Head 1966
Printed and bound in Great Britain for
The Bodley Head Ltd
9 Bow Street, London, WC2
by William Clowes & Sons Ltd, Beccles
Set in Monotype Baskerville
First published 1966
Reprinted 1970

Contents

Contents

Contents

Contents

Contents

Introduction

These traditional rhymes and games, some of them as old as social man, have a hint of poetry and magic in them. We remember them because they *are* memorable, because we heard them in childhood and we enjoy sharing them in turn with our own children.

Most of us know a good many of these rhymes, but unless we have used them continuously, memory plays tricks: we remember the whole vaguely; some lines are on the tip of the tongue but there are tantalizing gaps. And the actions that go with them? It is difficult to remember exactly how they go. What book can we consult to refresh our memory? So far as I know there is no one book where we can quickly find what we want, so that is the reason for *This Little Pig Went to Market*. It contains the very first rocking, tickling, and face-tapping games to be played with babies; finger plays; the more boisterous bouncing and other games for young children; and a short section of singing games and counting rhymes. All have directions which I hope are clear and easy to follow.

Play rhymes have been a tradition in my family. My own first recollection is hearing and playing them with my great-grandmother, and just recently, while compiling this book, I have had the fun of playing them with my grandchildren. I have given the versions we used, but every family has its own tradition, so I have given variants where I found them well established, and frequently a Scottish and an English version.

Too often I think we wait to *read* nursery rhymes to our children instead of beginning by singing or repeating them with actions to the words. To play with a baby, book in hand, is impossible. The only thing to do is to learn a few of the rhymes by heart. They are simple to learn, and certainly the baby will not notice if at first one's repertoire is small. Children, even the youngest, like the games to be played with precision. They soon come to expect the words and actions to be always the same; they like the formality and the ritual of expression; it gives them a comforting feeling of security.

The repetition of the words, the pattern of the rhyme, actually encourages a baby to try to talk. The actions illustrate the abstract words more vividly than any pictures. He watches and listens, and in the end, he joins in. He is responding to, co-operating with, others in a way that has linked one generation with another over the centuries. The counting rhymes may not teach a child to count; they do give him an interest in the numbers and an assurance that counting can be fun. I have put in the simplest of singing games which children enjoy as soon as they can walk and talk. Such games are played in many nursery schools, for they encourage the shyest child to join in, sure of a hand to hold and something definite to do.

Making this book has been a very great pleasure, and I would like to thank my family and friends for all the generous help they have given, especially Miss Kathleen Lines, who suggested the book. To Iona and Peter Opie, who have allowed me to include their family version of the tickling rhyme, *Round about, round about, here sits the hare*, from their famous *Dictionary of Nursery Rhymes*. Also to The Hogarth Press for their permission to use material from *The Hogarth Book of Scottish Nursery Rhymes*, collected and edited by my husband and me. Last but not least, the publishers for their patience and encouragement. I hope many will share the fun we have all had.

If this book becomes worn-out through constant family use it will have justified itself and our hopes for it.

NORAH MONTGOMERIE

This Little Pig Went to Market

Toe and Finger Counting

With the baby on your lap, take each bare toe in turn and give it a little shake, beginning with the big toe and progressing to the smallest one. End the game by running your fingers up the baby's leg and tickling his middle.

THIS little pig went to market,
This little pig stayed at home,
This little pig had roast beef,
This little pig had none,
And this little pig cried,
'Wee-wee-wee-wee-wee-wee,'
All the way home!

Toe and Finger Counting

THIS pig got into the barn,
This ate all the corn,
This said he wasn't well,
This said he'd go and tell,
And this said—'Squeak! squeak! squeak!
I can't get over the barn door sill.'

SEE-SAW, Margery Daw,
The hen flew over the malt house,
She counted her chickens one by one,
Still she missed the little white one,
Here it is, here it is, here it is!

WHOSE little pigs are these, these, these?
Whose little pigs are these?
They're Roger the Cook's,
I know by their looks;
And I found them among my peas.
Go pound them, go pound them.
I dare not on my life,
For though I love not Roger,
I dearly love his wife.

Toe and Finger Counting

In these rhymes, the little toe is counted first.

WEE Wiggie,
Poke Piggie,
Tom Whistle,
John Gristle
And old BIG GOBBLE, gobble, gobble!

'LET us go to the wood,' said this pig.
'What to do there?' said that pig.
'To look for my mother,' said this pig.
'What to do with her?' said that pig.
'Fetch her home, fetch her home!' said this pig.

The next four are finger-counting rhymes, the first two from
England, the other two from Scotland.

THIS little cow eats grass,
This little cow eats hay,
This little cow looks over the hedge,
This little cow runs away,
And this BIG cow does nothing at all
But lie in the fields all day!
We'll chase her,
     And chase her,
          And chase her!

Toe and Finger Counting

Master Thumb is first to come,
Then Pointer, steady and strong,
Then Tall Man high,
And just near by,
The Feeble Man does linger.
And last of all,
So neat and small,
Comes little Pinky Finger.

This is the man that broke the barn,
This is the man that stealt the corn,
This is the man that ran awa,
This is the man that telt all,
And poor Pirlie-winkie paid for all, paid for all.

Thumb bold,
Tibbity-told,
Langman,
Lickpan,
And Mammy's wee,
Wee man.

Tickling

With your finger, trace a circle round and round the palm of the baby's outstretched hand. Make the steps up his arm, and tickle him underneath it.

ROUND and round the garden
Went the teddy bear.
One step, two step,
Tickle you under there!

ROUND and round ran the wee hare.
One jump! Two jumps!
Tickle you under there.

ROUND about there
Sat the little hare.
The dogs came and chased him
Right up there!

Tickling

ROUND about the rosebush,
 Three steps,
 Four steps,
All the little boys and girls
Are sitting
On the doorsteps.

THERE was a wee mouse,
And he had a wee house,
And he lived up there.

Then he gaed creepy-crappy,
Creepy-crappy,
And made a hole in there.

Tickling

Pussy cat, pussy cat,
Where have you been?
I've been to London
To see the Queen.

Pussy cat, pussy cat,
What did you there?
I chased a little mouse
Under her chair.

Cheetie Pussie,
Catch a mousie,
Running through
Her little housie.

Pussie, catch
The little mousie,
Running through
Her little housie.

Tickling

HICKORY, dickory, dock!
The mouse ran up the clock,
The clock struck one,
Down the mouse run,
Hickory, dickory, dock!

Hickory, dickory, dare!
The pig flew up in the air,
The man in brown
Soon brought him down,
Hickory, dickory, dare!

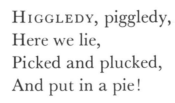

HIGGLEDY, piggledy,
Here we lie,
Picked and plucked,
And put in a pie!

DINGTY diddlety,
My mammy's maid,
She stole oranges,
I'm afraid.
Some in her pocket,
Some up her sleeve,
She stole oranges,
I do believe.

Tickling

ROUND about, round about,
   here sits the hare,
In the corner of a cornfield
   and that's just there.
     [*close to the thumb*]
This little dog found her,
[*fingers, starting with the thumb*]
This little dog ran her,
This little dog caught her,
This little dog ate her,
And this little dog said,
    'Give me a little bit, please'.

Tickling

After your fingers have crept up the baby's arm for the first
verse, they creep down to his hand again for the second.

ADAM and Eve gaed up my sleeve,
To fetch me down some candy.

Adam and Eve came down my sleeve,
And said there was none till Monday.

ROON aboot, roon aboot,
Catch a wee moose,
Up a bit, up a bit,
In a wee hoose.

There was a moose,
For want of stairs,
Cam doon a rope
To say his prayers.

Tickling

And here is another tickling rhyme, from Scotland, to play with a very small baby. As the baby lies on his back kicking his legs, tickle him by poking him gently with your thumb:

> THERE was a man,
> In Muir of Skene,
> He had dirks
> And I had none;
> But I fell on him
> With my thumbs,
> And wot you how,
> I dirkit him,
> Dirkit him,
> Dirkit him?

Tickling

These hand-tickling rhymes are for the slightly older child.
While his hand is being tickled the child is supposed to keep a
straight face, or else . . . according to the rhyme.

CAN you keep a secret?
I don't suppose you can.
Don't laugh and don't cry
While it tickles in your hand.

LADY, lady, in the land,
Can you bear a tickly hand?
If you laugh or if you smile,
You cannot be a lady.

IF YOU are a gentleman
As I suppose you be,
You'll neither laugh nor smile
At the tickling of your knee.

TICKLY, tickly, in your hand,
If you laugh you'll be a man,
If you smile you'll be a lady,
If you cry you'll be a baby.

Foot Patting

With the baby on your knee, pat the sole of one foot, then the other, in time with the words.

PITTY, patty, polt,
Shoe the wild colt!
Here a nail,
There a nail,
Pitty, patty, polt!

Foot Patting

'JOHN Smith, fellow fine,
Can you shoe this horse of mine?'
'Aye, sir, and that I can,
As well as ony man!
There's a nail upon the tae,
To make the pony climb the brae,
There's a nail upon the heel,
To help the pony pace well;
There's a nail, and there's a brod,
There's a horsie well shod.'

Is JOHN Smith within?
Yes, that he is.
Can he set a shoe?
Aye, marry, two;
Here a nail
And there a nail,
Tick, tack, too.

Foot Patting

SHOE a little horse,
Shoe a little mare,
But let the little colt
Go bare, bare, bare.

HOB, shoe, hob,
Hob, shoe, hob.
Here a nail,
There a nail,
And that's well shod.

Foot Patting

Tit, tat, toe,
My first go,
Three jolly butcher boys,
All in a row.

Stick one up,
Stick one down,
Stick one in
The old man's crown.

Foot Patting

THIS old man, he played one,
He played nick-nack on my drum,
Nick-nack, paddy-wack,
Give a dog a bone,
This old man went rolling home.

This old man, he played two,
He played nick-nack on my shoe,
Nick-nack, paddy-wack,
Give a dog a bone,
This old man went rolling home.

This old man, he played three,
He played nick-nack on my knee,
Nick-nack, paddy-wack,
Give a dog a bone,
This old man went rolling home.

This old man, he played four,
He played nick-nack on my door,
Nick-nack, paddy-wack,
Give a dog a bone,
This old man went rolling home.

This old man, he played five,
He played nick-nack on my hive,
Nick-nack, paddy-wack,
Give a dog a bone,
This old man went rolling home.

Foot Patting

This old man, he played six,
He played nick-nack on my sticks,
Nick-nack, paddy-wack,
Give a dog a bone,
This old man went rolling home.

This old man, he played seven,
He played nick-nack up to heaven,
Nick-nack, paddy-wack,
Give a dog a bone,
That old man went rolling HOME.

Having tapped the baby's feet as in the other rhymes, you can
pat his back, as though clapping a sack on it, and offer a cupped
hand, as though giving a handful of grain. End the game by
bouncing the baby up and down on your knee.

SHOE the pony, shoe,
Shoe the wild mare,
Put a sack upon her back
And see if she will bear!

If she will bear
We'll give her some grain,
If she'll not bear
We'll drive her again.

Rocking

Most rocking games are played with the baby sitting facing you on your lap. Hold both his hands and gently rock backwards and forwards.

SEE-SAW, Margery Daw,
Johnny shall have a new master,
He shall have but a penny a day,
Because he can't work any faster.

See-saw, Jack in the hedge,
Which is the way to London Bridge?
Put on your shoes and away you trudge,
That is the way to London Bridge.

Rocking

OH DEAR, what can the matter be?
Oh dear, what can the matter be?
Oh dear, what can the matter be?
Johnny's so long at the fair.

He promised to buy me a basket of posies,
A garland of lilies, a garland of roses,
He promised to buy me a bunch of blue ribbons,
To tie up my bonny brown hair.

Rocking

Up and down again,
On the counterpane,
High and dry and steady.
Baby rides on Mammy's knee,
Until her breakfast's ready.

Then she has her pap,
On her Daddy's lap,
Warm and snug and cosy.
If she's good and takes her food,
She'll grow up fat and rosy.

Dance a baby diddy,
What can mammy do wid'e?
Sit in her lap,
Give you some pap,
And dance a baby diddy!

Dormy, dormy, dormouse,
Sleeps in his little house.
He won't wake up
Till supper-time,
And that won't be
Till half-past nine.

Rocking

Then there are the lullaby rocking rhymes where the baby is
cradled in your arms.

ROCK-A-BYE baby, on the tree top,
When the wind blows, the cradle will rock,
When the bough breaks, the cradle will fall,
Down will come baby, cradle and all.

ROCK-A-BYE baby, your cradle is green,
Father's a king and mother's a queen,
Betty's a lady and wears a gold ring,
Johnnie's a drummer and drums for the king.

CATCH him crow, catch him kite!
Take him away till the apples are ripe,
When the apples are ripe and ready to fall,
Down comes baby, apples and all.

Rocking

HUSH-A-BYE, baby,
Daddy's away,
Brothers and sisters
Have gone out to play;
But here by your cradle,
Dear baby, I'll keep,
To guard you from danger,
And sing you to sleep.

Hush-a-bye, baby,
Pussy's a lady,
Mousie has gone to the mill,
And if you don't cry
She'll come back by and by,
So hush-a-bye, baby, lie still.

Rocking

DIDDLE-me-diddle-me-dandy-O!
Diddle-me-diddle-me-darlin.
If I ever bake a sugar cake,
I'll bake little baby a parkin.

HOOLIE, the bed'll fall!
Wha'll fall with it?
Two eyes, two hands,
And two bonnie feet.

Hoolie, the bed'll not fall!
Wha'll not fall with it?
Wee Robin Redbreast,
Sound asleep.

Leg Wagging

With the baby sitting comfortably on your knee with his back to you, take each leg by the ankle and lift one over the other in turn, to the rhythm of the first three lines of the rhyme. At 'Jump!' lift up both legs. This usually makes the baby topple back against you and causes much amusement.

LEG over leg,
As the dog goes to Dover,
When he comes to a wall,
Jump! He goes over!

SEE-SAW, sacradown,
Which is the way to London town?
One foot up and one foot down,
That is the way to London Town.

UP AND down the market,
Selling penny buns,
One a penny, two a penny,
Three a penny buns!

Leg Wagging

With the baby on your knee, hold his legs and work them up and down in a walking movement, repeating the first two lines of the rhyme. At the third line, dip one leg to the right, then one leg to the left. Repeating the sequence line by line, rapidly dip one leg after the other. Finally, gallop the baby on your knee, faster and faster, to the end of the rhyme.

THE doggies gaed to the mill,
This way and that way,
They took a lick out of this wife's poke,
They took a lick out of that wife's poke,
And a loup in the laid and a dip in the dam,
And gaed walloping, walloping, walloping hame.

Leg Wagging

Two leg-wagging rhymes, useful when the baby is being undressed and does not want his shoes taken off. The first one comes from Scotland.

FEETIKIN, feetikin,
When will you gang?
When the nights turn short,
And the days turn lang,
I'll toddle and gang,
Toddle and gang!

DIDDLE, diddle, dumpling, my son John,
Went to bed with his trousers on;
One shoe off and one shoe on,
Diddle, diddle, dumpling, my son John.

Leg Wagging

With the baby sitting on your lap, take both his legs by the ankles, and name one 'Bill Anderson' and the other 'Tom Sim'. Lift one leg over the other in turn, faster and faster, until the last line. Then part your knees and allow the baby to slip down between them.

THIS is Bill Anderson,
That is Tom Sim.
Tom called Bill to fight,
And fell over him.
Bill over Tom,
And Tom over Bill,
Over and over as
They fell down the hill.

Leg Wagging

With the baby sitting on your lap, take hold of his legs and
work them up and down for the first five lines of the rhyme. At
'Here we go down' part your knees just enough to allow the
baby's legs to slip between them. Pulling them up again, rock
the baby to and fro until the last two lines, when you hold up
each leg in turn.

HEY my kitten, my kitten,
Hey my kitten, my dearie,
Sic a foot as this
Is na far nor nearie.
Here we go up, up, up,
Here we go down, down, downie,
Here we go back and fore,
Here we go round and roundie;
Here's a leg for a stocking,
And here's a foot for a shoe-ie!

Leg Wagging

With the baby sitting on your knee, take both his legs and work them up and down in time with the rhyme, faster and faster until the last line. At 'jumped' lift up both legs as high as they will go.

OLD Farmer Giles,
He went seven miles,
With his faithful dog, Rover.
Old Farmer Giles,
When he came to stiles,
Took a run and jumped over!

Face Tapping

Repeating the rhyme and miming the words, tap the baby's forehead, and then each part of his face in turn. For the latch raise his nose with one hand and, with the other, pop his fingers into his own mouth. The game ends with taps on his chin and tickles down to his middle.

BROW bender,
Eye peeper,
Nose dreeper,
Mouth eater,
Chin chopper,
Knock at the door,
Ring the bell,
Lift up the latch,
Walk in . . .
Take a chair
And sit down there,
How do you do,
And how do you do,
And how do you do again?

Face Tapping

Brow, brow, brenty,
Ee, ee, winky,
Nose, nose, nebbie,
Cheek, cheek, cherry,
Mou, mou, merrie,
Chin, chin, chackie,
Catch a fly,
    Catch a fly,
        Catch a fly!

Knock at the door,
Ring the bell,
Peep through the keyhole,
Lift up the latch,
Wipe your shoes,
Walk in,
Chin, chin, chin, chopper.

Here is a Scottish rhyme for the baby's teeth and tongue:

Four and twenty white kye,
Standing in a stall,
By came the reid bull,
And licked them all.

Face Tapping

Repeating the words of the rhyme, touch the baby's forehead at 'Farmer Giles', his eyes at 'his two men', his nose at 'the cockadoodle', his mouth at 'the hen', and his teeth at 'the little chickens'. The game ends by tapping his chin with sharp little chopping movements.

HERE sits Farmer Giles,
Here sit his two men,
Here sits the cockadoodle,
Here sits the hen,
Here sit the little chickens,
Here they run in,
Chin chopper, chin chopper,
Chin, chin, chin.

Face Tapping

Holding the baby's nose between the finger and thumb of one hand, 'chop' it off with the other.

MY MOTHER and your mother
Went over the way,
Said your mother to my mother,
It's chop-a-nose day!

In this Scottish rhyme, tapping begins with the baby's toes and ends with tickles over his head and down his back.

TAE titty,
Wee fitty,
Shin chappy,
Knee nappy,
Hinchie pinchie
Wymie bulgy,
Breast berry,
Moo merry,
Neb nappy,
Eye winkie,
Broo brinkie,
Ower the croon,
Doon we go,
    doon we go,
        doon we go!

Finger Play

Hold up your hand for the baby to see, then, repeating the first two lines, waggle the thumb, at the same time tucking the four fingers into the palm of your hand, out of sight. At 'Dance, you merry men', waggle all fingers along with the thumb, which dances alone again for the last two lines.

Repeating the first two lines of the second verse, waggle your forefinger, and the pattern of the game is repeated as before, according to the words.

This is repeated with the middle finger, ring finger, and little finger, the actions always suiting the words of the rhyme.

DANCE, thumbkin, dance,
Dance, thumbkin, dance,
Dance, you merry men, every one;
But thumbkin, he can dance alone,
Thumbkin, he can dance.

Finger Play

Dance, foreman, dance,
Dance, foreman, dance,
Dance, you merry men, every one,
But foreman, he can dance alone,
Foreman, he can dance.

Dance, middleman, dance,
Dance, middleman, dance,
Dance, you merry men, every one,
But middleman, he can dance alone,
Middleman, he can dance.

Dance, ringman, dance,
Dance, ringman, dance,
Dance, you merry men, every one,
But ringman, he can dance alone,
Ringman, he can dance.

Littleman, he can dance,
Littleman, he can dance,
Dance, you merry men, every one,
Littleman, he can dance alone,
Littleman, he can dance.

Finger Play

I know of no actions for these next two finger plays, and I suggest that you invent your own actions to suit the words.

I HAD a little husband,
No bigger than my thumb,
I put him in a pint pot,
And there made him drum.

I gave him some garters,
To garter up his hose,
And a little pocket handkerchief,
To wipe his little nose.

I HAD a little manikin,
I set him on my thumbikin,
I saddled him, I bridled him,
And sent him to the Townikin.

I bought a pair of garters
To tie his wee bit hosikin,
I bought a pocket handkerchief
To dight his wee bit nosikin;

I sent him to the garden
To fetch a pound of sage,
And found him in the kitchen nook,
Kissing little Madge.

Finger Play

With a piece of paper stuck on both index fingers, tuck your other fingers into the palm of each hand, the backs facing the baby. Stick up both index fingers, naming one 'Peter' and the other 'Paul'. At 'Fly away', toss each appropriate hand over your shoulder, out of sight, bringing it back immediately, with the middle finger in place of the index finger, and the paper nowhere to be seen. All very mysterious to anyone under four years of age.

Two little dicky birds,
Sitting on a wall,
One named Peter,
One named Paul.
Fly away, Peter!
Fly away, Paul!
Come back, Peter!
Come back, Paul!

With the tip of your right forefinger touching the left thumb, twist your hands so that the left forefinger touches the right thumb and so on, making them climb up above your head in half circles.

At 'Down came the rain' let your arms fall; at 'Washed' part your hands with a sweep; at 'Out came the sun' raise your arms above your head and make an arc, raising them again at 'dried up all the rain'. The game ends by repeating the climbing movement as the spider climbs 'up the spout again'.

Incey, wincey spider, climbed up the spout,
Down came the rain, and washed the spider out;
Out came the sun, and dried up all the rain;
Incey, wincey spider, climbed up the spout again.

Finger Play

Sit beside the baby and hold up both your hands for him to see. Place the parted thumb and finger-tips of one hand against those of the other, rounding them and drawing the wrists together to make a 'ball', and encourage the baby to do the same. Continue to make your actions suit the words; hold up your straightened fingers for soldiers, clap for the music, mime playing the trumpet, play hide-and-seek behind your hands, put one hand on top of your other fingers for the umbrella, and for the cradle interlock the fingers of both hands and rock gently.

HERE is a ball for baby,
Big and soft and round,
Here is baby's hammer,
See how he can pound.

Here are baby's soldiers
Standing in a row,
Here is baby's music,
Clapping, clapping so!

Here is baby's trumpet,
Tootle-tootle-oo,
Here is the way baby
Plays 'peek-a-boo'!

Here's a big umbrella
To keep the baby dry;
Here is baby's cradle,
Rock-a-baby-bye.

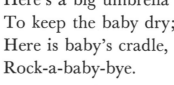

Finger Play

Place your knuckles together and interlace your fingers. With the palms up, make both hands flat, the interlacing fingers lying side by side, like knives and forks. At the second line, turn your hands over, dropping the wrists, making a 'table' with the interlaced fingers. At the third line, raise both index fingers, tip to tip to make a 'looking glass', and at the fourth line, also raise both little fingers, tip to tip. The hands are then rocked like a cradle.

HERE are the lady's knives and forks,
Here is the lady's table,
Here is the lady's looking-glass,
And here is the baby's cradle.
Rock-rock, rock-rock, rock-rock.

Finger Play

Hold up both hands for the baby to see, the palms towards you,
fingers together, thumbs well separated. Cross one wrist over
the other, interlocking the thumbs, and making your outstretched fingers flap like the wings of a bird, while repeating the
first three lines of the rhyme. At 'flies away', lift your hands,
still flapping, as high as you can.

THIS little bird flaps its wings,
Flaps its wings, flaps its wings,
This little bird flaps its wings,
And flies away in the morning!

HERE'S a string of wild geese,
How many for a penny?
One for my lord,
And one for my lady.
Up the gate and down the gate,
They're all flown from me.

Finger Play

Hop two fingers of one hand in front of the baby, coming to a halt at the last 'stop'. Walk two fingers of your other hand towards them, waggling your thumb at 'How do you do'. Shake a finger of your first hand, which you then lift above your head, fingers fluttering, for the final line.

ONCE I saw a little bird
Come hop, hop, hop.
I cried, 'Little bird,
Will you stop, stop, stop!'

I went to the window,
Saying, 'How do you do?'
But he shook his little tail,
And away he flew.

And two more rhymes using your hands to fit the words.

ROBIN, Robin, Redbreast,
Sits on a rail;
He nods with his head,
And wags with his tail.

Finger Play

A LITTLE cock sparrow sat on a green tree,
He chirruped and chirruped, so merry was he.
A naughty boy came with his wee bow and arrow,
Determined to shoot the little cock sparrow.

'This little sparrow shall make me a stew,
And his giblets shall make me a little pie, too!'
'Oh no,' said the sparrow, 'I won't make a stew.'
So he flapped his wings and away he flew.

Finger Play

For the first line, interlock your fingers and enclose them in the cupped palms of your hands, your knuckles uppermost to suggest the pitched roof of a church. Keep the thumbs upright and close together.

At the second line, raise both index fingers and hold them tip to tip, to suggest a steeple, the upright thumbs representing the main doors.

At the third line, open the 'doors', and at the fourth, turn the hands inside out, showing a somewhat restless congregation of fingers.

HERE is the church,
And here is the steeple,
Open the doors,
And here are all the people.

Undo your hands, cross your wrists and, with the hands back to back, interlace the two little fingers, the third fingers, the middle fingers, and finally the index fingers, repeating the first two lines of the next verse as you do it.

The action for the last lines requires some dexterity; while keeping your fingers interlaced, drop your hands forward, bring your palms together by folding your left hand under your left arm, so that the thumbs are facing upwards. Wrap the outer thumb round the inner thumb, which now sticks up like a minister in a pulpit.

Here is the parson,
Going upstairs,
And here is the parson,
Saying his prayers.

Finger Play

If you can bear to keep your hands in this awkward position, you can make the minister deliver a sermon by waggling your thumb. End the game with your hands falling into your lap.

Dearly beloved brethren, is it not a sin,
When you peel potatoes to throw away the skin?
For the skin feeds pigs, and the pigs feed you,
Dearly beloved brethren, is this not true?

The stairs gave a crack,
The parson broke his back,
And all the naughty little boys
Cried: 'Quack! quack! quack!'

In Scotland they say:

The meenister in the poopit,
He couldna say his prayers,
He laughed and he giggled,
And fell doon the stairs.
The stairs gave a crack,
And he broke his humphy back
And all the congregation said,
'Quack, quack, quack!'

Finger Play

Tucking your fingers into your palms, hold up both hands. Then, keeping the palms turned towards you, raise one thumb and waggle it as you repeat the first four lines of the first verse. Continuing, raise the first finger at 'he had two', the second at 'three little', and so on, until all ten fingers are raised. Then, one by one, each finger is tucked back into the palm again.

Old Davy Jones had one little sailor,
Old Davy Jones had one little sailor,
Old Davy Jones had one little sailor,
    One little sailor boy.
He had one, he had two, he had three little sailors,
Four little, five little, six little sailors,
Seven little, eight little, nine little sailors,
    Ten little sailor boys.

Old Davy Jones had ten little sailors,
Old Davy Jones had ten little sailors,
Old Davy Jones had ten little sailors,
    Ten little sailor boys.
He had ten, he had nine, he had eight little sailors,
Seven little, six little, five little sailors,
Four little, three little, two little sailors,
    One little sailor boy.

Finger Play

Hold up your forearm and allow the hand to hang from the wrist. Repeating the first verse, slowly creep the fingers of the other hand up the back of your hanging hand. Pause for the second verse, and creep down the forearm for the third:

THE bear went over the mountain,
The bear went over the mountain,
The bear went over the mountain,
To see what he could see.

(And what do you think he saw?)

The other side of the mountain,
The other side of the mountain,
The other side of the mountain,
Was all that he could see.

So the bear went over the mountain,
The bear went over the mountain,
The bear went over the mountain,
So very happily.

Finger Play

With the baby sitting in his high chair, hold up both hands for him to see. Repeating the first line, flutter all ten fingers in a bird-like movement. At 'One flew away', toss both hands above your head, bringing them down again with one finger tucked into the palm, out of sight, leaving nine fingers which are fluttered for the first line of the second verse, and so on.

This pattern is repeated with each finger in turn, to the last line of the rhyme, when NO fingers, or 'chickadees', are to be seen.

TEN little chickadees sitting on a line,
One flew away and then there were nine.

Nine little chickadees on a farmer's gate,
One flew away and then there were eight.

Eight little chickadees looking up to heaven,
One flew away and then there were seven.

Seven little chickadees gathering up sticks,
One flew away and then there were six.

Six little chickadees learning how to dive,
One flew away and then there were five.

Five little chickadees sitting at a door
One flew away and then there were four.

Four little chickadees could not agree,
One flew away and then there were three.

Finger Play

Three little chickadees looking very blue,
One flew away and then there were two.

Two little chickadees sitting in the sun,
One flew away and then there was one.

One little chickadee living all alone,
He flew away and then there was NONE!

Finger Play

TEN little Injuns standing in a line,
One toddled home and then there were nine,
Nine little Injuns swingin' on a gate,
One tumbled off and then there were eight.

One little, two little, three little, four little,
Five little Injun boys,
Six little, seven little, eight little, nine little,
Ten little Injun boys.

Eight little Injuns gayest under heaven,
One went to sleep and then there were seven,
Seven little Injuns, up to their tricks,
One broke his neck and then there were six.

One little, two little, three little, four little,
Five little Injun boys,
Six little, seven little, eight little, nine little,
Ten little Injun boys.

Six little Injuns playing with a hive,
A bumble-bee stung one and then there were five,
Five little Injuns at a cellar door,
One fell in and then there were four.

Finger Play

One little, two little, three little, four little,
Five little Injun boys,
Six little, seven little, eight little, nine little,
Ten little Injun boys.

Four little Injuns up on a spree,
One he got fuddled and then there were three,
Three little Injuns out in a canoe,
One tumbled overboard and then there were two.

One little, two little, three little, four little,
Five little Injun boys,
Six little, seven little, eight little, nine little,
Ten little Injun boys.

Two little Injuns foolin' with a gun,
One shot the other and then there was one,
One little Injun livin' all alone,
He got married and then there were none.

One little, two little, three little, four little,
Five little Injun boys,
Six little, seven little, eight little, nine little,
Ten little Injun boys.

Finger Play

This time hold up both hands, allowing the fingers to hang down, representing ten bottles, and keeping the backs of your hands towards the baby. Hold them in this position until the word 'fall', when they are allowed to drop into your lap. Quickly bring them up again with a finger tucked out of sight, leaving nine hanging down. This is repeated with each finger in turn, according to the words, until the last line of the last verse, when the hands remain on your lap, the fingers out of sight.

TEN green bottles hanging on the wall,
Ten green bottles hanging on the wall,
And if one green bottle should accidentally fall,
There'd be nine green bottles hanging on the wall.

Nine green bottles hanging on the wall, etc.

(and so on down to)

One green bottle hanging on the wall,
One green bottle hanging on the wall,
And if that green bottle should accidentally fall,
There'd be NO green bottles hanging there at all.

Finger Play

The actions for the rest of the rhymes in this section can be adapted to suit the verses.

ONE, two, kittens that mew,
Two, three, birds on a tree,
Three, four, shells on the shore,
Four, five, bees from the hive,
Five, six, the cow that licks,
Six, seven, rooks in the heaven,
Seven, eight, sheep at the gate,
Eight, nine, clothes on a line,
Nine, ten, the little black hen.

ONE, two, three, four, five,
Once I caught a fish alive,
Six, seven, eight, nine, ten,
Then I let it go again.
Why did I let it go?
Because it bit my finger so.
Which finger did it bite?
This little finger on the right.

Finger Play

THREE mice went into a hole to spin,
Puss passed by and she peeped in:
'What are you doing, my little men?'
'Weaving coats for gentlemen.'
'Please let me come in to wind off your thread.'
'Oh no, Mistress Pussy, you'll bite off our heads.'

Says Puss: 'You look so wondrous wise,
I like your whiskers and bright black eyes,
Your house is the nicest house I see,
I think there is room for you and me.'
The mice were so pleased that they opened the door,
And Pussy soon laid them all dead on the floor.

CHILDREN can hop on one leg,
Children can hop on two,
No one walks on three legs,
But Pussy walks on four.

Finger Play

LITTLE Miss Muffet,
She sat on a tuffet,
Eating her curds and whey;
Down came a spider,
And sat down beside her,
And frightened Miss Muffet away!

I LOVE little pussy,
Her coat is so warm,
And if I don't hurt her
She'll do me no harm.

So I'll not pull her tail,
Nor drive her away;
But pussy and I
Together will play.

She will sit by my side,
And I'll give her some food;
And she'll like me because
I'm so gentle and good.

Finger Play

LITTLE Jack Horner,
Sat in a corner,
Eating his Christmas Pie;
He put in his thumb,
And pulled out a plum,
And said, 'What a good boy am I!'

OH WHERE, oh where has my little dog gone,
Oh where, oh where can he be?
With his ears cut short and his tail cut long,
Oh where, oh where is he?

Finger Play

THERE was a crooked man,
And he went a crooked mile,
He found a crooked sixpence,
Beside a crooked stile;
He bought a crooked cat,
That caught a crooked mouse,
And they all lived together
In a little crooked house.

POLLY put the kettle on,
Polly put the kettle on,
Polly put the kettle on,
We'll all have tea.

Sukey take it off again,
Sukey take it off again,
Sukey take it off again,
They've all gone away.

Finger Play

Place the closed, outstretched fingers of one hand across the
outstretched fingers of the other, at right angles. Then separate
the first finger of each hand from the others, leaving a small hole.
Invite the child to put his finger into this hole, and when he does
so, gently nip it with both your thumbs underneath your fingers.

> Put your finger in Foxy's hole,
> Foxy's not at home;
> Foxy's at the back door
> Picking at a bone!

Clench one hand into a loose fist leaving a hole at the top. Invite the child to put his finger into the hole, then grasp it tightly
while the rhyme is being said, suddenly letting it pop out on the
last line.

> I put my finger in the woodpecker's hole,
> The woodpecker said, 'God bless my soul,
> 'Take it out,
> 'Take it out,
> 'Take it out,
> 'REMOVE IT!'

Hand Clapping

CLAP hands, clap hands,
Till father comes home,
For father's got money,
But mother's got none.

CLAP, clap handies,
Mammie's wee ain,
Clap, clap handies,
Daddy's coming hame,
Hame to his bonnie
Wee bit laddie,
Clap, clap handies.

HANDY pandy, Jack-a-dandy,
Loves plum cake and sugar candy,
He bought some at the grocer's shop,
And out he came, hop, hop, hop!

Hand Clapping

Show the baby how to clap his hands together rhythmically to the first two lines of the rhyme. At 'roll it', rub his hands together, then prick the palm of his left hand with his right forefinger, and trace a 'B' on it. End the game by tossing both hands outwards.

PAT-A-CAKE, pat-a-cake, baker's man,
Bake me a cake as fast as you can;
Roll it and prick it and mark it with B,
Toss in the oven for baby and me.

First hide something in one clenched fist. Then present both fists to your companion, one on top of the other. If he guesses correctly which hand the object is in, it is his turn to hide it next; otherwise he must guess again.

HANDY Pandy,
Sugar Candy,
Which one will you choose,
Top or bottom?

Hand Clapping

Nievie, nievie, nick, nack,
Which one will you tick-tak?
Tak one, tak twa,
Tak the best among them a'.

I'll tak this,
I'll tak that,
I'll tak nievie
Nick-nack!

This is a game, in which one child places his hand flat on the table, another child puts her hand on his, and so on, until all the players have both hands on the pile. Then the first child withdraws his hand from the bottom of the pile and puts it on the top, the second player does the same and so do the others, in sequence, one after the other, faster and faster, until the game ends in confusion.

Hot cross buns!
Hot cross buns!
One a penny, two a penny,
Hot cross buns!
If you have no daughters
Give them to your sons,
But if you haven't any of those pretty little elves
You cannot do better than eat them yourselves!

Hand Clapping

This clapping game is an excellent hand-warmer. Facing each other, two children clap hands in time with the rhyme, in this order: Clap their own hands—Clap right hands—Clap their own hands—Clap left hands—Clap their own hands—and clap both hands together. This sequence is repeated with increasing speed, until the game ends in confusion or sheer exhaustion.

PEASE pudding hot,
Pease pudding cold,
Pease pudding in the pot
Nine days old.

Some like it hot,
Some like it cold,
Some like it in the pot
Nine days old.

Jig Jogging

These rhymes have the rhythm that helps you to keep up the endless knee jig-jogging demanded by a tireless child rider.

With the child seated on your crossed leg, jump him up and down in time with the words, and with actions that suit them.

RIDE a cock-horse, to Banbury Cross,
To see a fine lady ride on a white horse;
Rings on her fingers and bells on her toes,
She shall have music wherever she goes.

RIDE a cock-horse,
To Banbury Cross,
To see what Tommy can buy;
A penny loaf, a penny white cake,
And a tuppenny apple pie.

TO MARKET, to market, to buy a fat pig,
Home again, home again, jiggety-jig!
To market, to market, to buy a fat hog,
Home again, home again, jiggety-jog!

Jig Jogging

In Scotland they say:

THE cattie rade to Paisley, to Paisley, to Paisley,
The cattie rade to Paisley upon a harrow tine,
And she came louping hame again,
And she came louping hame again,
Upon a mare of mine.
It was upon a Wednesday,
A windy, windy Wednesday,
It was upon a Wednesday,
Gin I can rightly mind.

TROT, trot, horsie,
Going away to Fife,
Coming back on Monday
With a new wife.

And somewhere near the Wash, they say:

TRIT trot to Boston,
Trit trot to Lynn,
Take care, little boy,
And don't fall in!

Jig Jogging

Hey diddle dinky, poppety, pet,
The merchants of London, they wear scarlet,
Silk on the collar and gold on the hem,
So merrily march the merchant-men.

Ride away, ride away, baby shall ride,
And have a wee puppy-dog tied to one side,
A wee pussy-cat shall be tied to the other,
And baby shall ride to see her grandmother.

Gee up, my horse, to Buddleigh Fair,
What shall we do when we get there?
Candy and fruits and red sugar balls,
Roundabout riding and coconut stalls.

Rub-a-dub-dub,
Three men in a tub,
And who do you think they be?
The butcher, the baker,
The candlestick-maker,
Turn them out, knaves all three!

Hippity-hop to the sweetie shop,
To buy a stick of candy,
One for you, and one for me,
And one for sister Mandy.

Jig Jogging

LITTLE Johnny Morgan,
Gentleman of Wales,
Came riding on a nanny-goat,
Selling pigs' tails.

With the child on your knee, trot him up and down, miming
the rhyme and encouraging him to mime, too. The game ends
with a high-pitched imitation of a train whistle.

DOWN at the station, early every morning,
  Two little puff-puffs, all in a row.
Man on the engine, turns a little handle,
  Chuff-chuff-chuff, and away we go!
  Chuff-chuff-chuffchuff,
  Chuff-chuff-chuffchuff,
  Chuff-chuff-chuffchuff,
  Ooooooooooooooooooooooooo . . . .!

Jig Jogging

With the child seated on your crossed legs, jump him up and down, gently at first, but with increasing vigour, to suit the words of the rhyme. At 'he falls in a ditch', he is allowed to slip down to the ground.

THIS is the way the ladies ride,
    Nimble nimm, nimble nimm,
This is the way the gentlemen ride,
    A gallop a trot, a gallop a trot,
This is the way the farmers ride,
    Jiggety jog, jiggety jog,
This is the way the butcher boy rides,
    Tripperty trot, tripperty trot,
Till he falls in a ditch with a flipperty,
    Flipperty, flop, flop, FLOP!

HERE goes my lord,
    A trot, a trot, a trot, a trot,
Here goes my lady,
    A canter, a canter, a canter, a canter,
Here goes my young master,
    Jockey-hitch, jockey-hitch, jockey-hitch, jockey-hitch,
Here goes my young miss,
    An amble, an amble, an amble, an amble,
The footman lags behind to tipple ale and wine,
And goes a gallop, a gallop, to make up his time.

Jig Jogging

HERE comes a lady, with her little baby,
 A nim, a nim, a nim,
Here come my lord, with his trusty sword,
 Trot, trot, trot,
Here comes old Jack with a broken pack,
 A gallop, a gallop, a gallop!

I HAVE a little pony,
His name is Dapple Grey,
I lent him to a lady,
To ride a mile away.

She lashed him and whipped him,
She rode him through the mire,
I would not lend my pony now,
For all the lady's hire.

I love my little pony,
He's safely carried me,
And corn, and hay, and stable,
Is all he's asked for fee.

I've saddled him and ridden him
Many a summer's day,
And no one shall treat unkindly,
My little Dapple Grey.

Jig Jogging

With the baby seated on your knee, jog him up and down for the first two lines of the rhyme. At 'Father fell off', let him slip down to the right, and at 'Mother fell off', let him slip down to the left. Then pull him back on to your knee, trotting him faster and faster, like Uncle John, to the end of the rhyme.

FATHER and Mother and Uncle John,
Went to market, one by one,
Father fell off!
Mother fell off!
But Uncle John went on, and on,
And on, and on and on.

Jig Jogging

JOHN Cook had a little grey mare,
      He, haw, hum!
Her back stood up and her bones were bare,
      He, haw, hum!

John Cook was riding up Shuter's Bank,
      He, haw, hum!
And there his nag did kick and prank,
      He, haw, hum!

John Cook was riding up Shuter's Hill,
      He, haw, hum!
His mare fell down and she made her will,
      He, haw, hum!

The bridle and saddle he laid on the shelf,
      He, haw, hum!
If you want any more you can sing it yourself,
      He, haw, hum!

Jig Jogging

Yankee Doodle came to town,
Upon a little pony,
He stuck a feather in his cap,
And called it Macaroni.

First he bought a porridge pot,
And then he bought a ladle,
And then he trotted home again,
As fast as he was able.

Yankee Doodle is a tune
That comes in mighty handy,
All the bad boys run away
At Yankee Doodle dandy.

Yankee Doodle, doodle doo,
Yankee doodle dandy,
All the lassies are so smart
And sweet as sugar candy.

Jig Jogging

This is a great favourite north of the border. It was obviously made for bouncing a young child on one's knee.

DANCE to your daddie,
My bonnie laddie,
Dance to your daddie,
My bonnie lamb.

You shall get a fishie
In a little dishie,
And you'll get an eggie
And a bit of ham.

You shall get a coatie,
And a pair of breekies,
You shall get a fishie
When the boats come hame.

You shall get a pony
Fit to ride for ony,
And you'll get a whippie
For to make him gang.

Dance to your daddie
My bonnie laddie,
Dance to your daddie,
My bonnie lamb.

Jig Jogging

KATIE Beardie had a cow,
Black and white about the mou,
Wasna that a dainty cow?
　Dance, Katie Beardie!

Katie Beardie had a hen,
Cackled but and cackled ben,
Wasna that a dainty hen?
　Dance, Katie Beardie!

Katie Beardie had a cock,
That could spin, and bake, and rock,
Wasna that a dainty cock?
　Dance, Katie Beardie!

Katie Beardie had a grice,
It could skate upon the ice,
Wasna that a dainty grice?
　Dance, Katie Beardie!

Jig Jogging

Cock-a-doodle-doo!
My dame has lost her shoe,
My master's lost his fiddling stick,
And doesn't know what to do.

Cock-a-doodle-doo!
What is my dame to do?
Till master finds his fiddling stick,
She'll be without her shoe.

Cock-a-doodle-doo!
My dame has found her shoe,
And master's found his fiddling stick,
Sing Cock-a-doodle-doo!

Cock-a-doodle-doo!
My dame will dance with you,
While master fiddles his fiddling stick
For dame and doodle-doo!

Here am I, little Jumping Joan,
When nobody's with me
I'm always alone!

First Singing Games

The children join hands and dance round in a ring. At the end of the first verse, they fall down; at the end of the second, they kneel down, at the third—bow down—and finally at the very last line, they all fall down again.

A RING, a ring o' roses,
 A pocket full o' posies,
  A-tish-o! A-tish-o!
  All fall down!

A bird upon the steeple
 Sits high above the people,
  A-tish-o! A-tish-o!
  All kneel down!

The King has sent his daughter,
 To fetch a pail of water,
  A-tish-o! A-tish-o!
  All bow down!

The wedding bells are ringing,
 The boys and girls are singing,
  A-tish-o! A-tish-o!
  All fall DOWN!

First Singing Games

The children stand in a large circle round one child, who chooses a partner from the circle by dancing in front of him with a stiff, puppet-like movement, working his arms up and down, and singing:

> DO YOU know the Muffin Man,
> The Muffin Man, the Muffin Man?
> Do you know the Muffin Man
> Who lives in Drury Lane?

The partner replies with the same movements:

> Yes, I know the Muffin Man,
> The Muffin Man, the Muffin Man,
> Yes, I know the Muffin Man
> Who lives in Drury Lane.

These two children continue to make the puppet-like movements together, inside the circle which stands, singing:

> O, two know the Muffin Man,
> The Muffin Man, the Muffin Man,
> O, two know the Muffin Man
> Who lives in Drury Lane.

First Singing Games

The two inside the circle then face two *in* the circle, and sing: 'Do you know the Muffin Man?' The game is repeated, and continues until all are making the puppet-like movements and singing:

We all know the Muffin Man, etc.

Joining hands, the children form a ring round the Farmer, and dance round, singing:

THE Farmer in his den,
The Farmer in his den,
  Hey O, my daddy O,
The Farmer in his den.

The Farmer wants a Wife,
The Farmer wants a Wife,
  Hey O, my daddy O,
The Farmer wants a Wife.

The Farmer in the centre now chooses a Wife from the ring. She joins him in the middle, and the ring dances round them, singing:

The Wife wants a Child,
The Wife wants a Child,
Hey O, my daddy O,
The Wife wants a Child.

The Wife chooses a Child from the ring. The Child joins the two in the middle, and the ring dances round them, singing:

The Child wants a Nurse,
The Child wants a Nurse,
Hey O, my daddy O,
The Child wants a Nurse.

The Child chooses a Nurse from the ring. The Nurse joins the three in the middle, and the ring dances round them, singing:

The Nurse wants a Dog,
The Nurse wants a Dog,
Hey O, my daddy O,
The Nurse wants a Dog.

First Singing Games

The Nurse chooses a Dog from the ring. The Dog joins the four in the middle, and the ring continues:

> The Dog stands still,
> The Dog stands still,
>   Hey O, my daddy O,
> The Dog stands still.

The ring breaks up, and all the children pat the Dog, singing:

> We all pat the Dog,
> We all pat the Dog,
>   Hey O, my daddy O,
> We all pat the Dog.

The Dog now becomes the Farmer, and the game is repeated.

First Singing Games

The children join hands and dance round in a ring, singing the refrain: 'Here we go round the mulberry bush.' Then they stand still and mime the words of each alternate verse. Finally joining hands, they dance round again, singing the refrain.

HERE we go round the mulberry bush,
The mulberry bush, the mulberry bush,
Here we go round the mulberry bush,
On a fine and frosty morning.

This is the way we wash our hands,
Wash our hands, wash our hands,
This is the way we wash our hands,
On a fine and frosty morning.

Here we go round the mulberry bush, etc.

This is the way we dry our hands, etc.

This is the way we clap our hands, etc.

This is the way we stamp our feet, etc.

First Singing Games

In two rows, several paces apart, the players face each other. Holding hands, one line advances and retreats, singing the first verse, and stand as the others advance and retreat, answering with the second verse. From the other line, a player is chosen as 'nuts and may' by the first, who also choose one of themselves to 'pull her away'. The game is repeated until, through a series of these contests, all the players are in one line.

HERE we come gathering nuts and may,
Nuts and may, nuts and may,
Here we come gathering nuts and may,
On a cold and frosty morning.

Who will you have for nuts and may,
Nuts and may, nuts and may,
Who will you have for nuts and may,
On a cold and frosty morning?

We'll have ———— for nuts and may,
Nuts and may, nuts and may,
We'll have ———— for nuts and may,
On a cold and frosty morning.

Who will you send to pull her away,
To pull her away, pull her away,
Who will you send to pull her away,
On a cold and frosty morning?

We'll send ———— to pull her away,
To pull her away, pull her away,
We'll send ———— to pull her away,
On a cold and frosty morning.

First Singing Games

One child is chosen by the others to be their leader, then they all line up behind the leader, imitating his actions as he marches about the room.

WE ARE off to Timbuctoo,
Would you like to go there, too?
All the way and back again,
You must follow our leader then,
You must follow our leader,
You must follow our leader,
All the way and back again,
You must follow our leader.

Another 'follow the leader' rhyme and game, but this time the children hold on to the preceding child's dress or jersey.

POLLY Perkin, hold on to my jerkin,
Hold on to my gown,
That's the way we march to town.

First Singing Games

The children run about while one of them tries to catch another as he or she calls out:

> I'M THE wee mouse
> In a hole in the wall,
> And I've come out
> To catch you all!

When the 'mouse' catches one of the players, they hold hands and together try to catch a third. Each child caught joins the chain until, one by one, all have been caught. By the way, no one can be caught while the chain is broken.

First Singing Games

The children join hands in a circle and walk round, singing:

> WHEN I was a baby,
> A baby, a baby,
> When I was a baby,
> How happy was I.

They stand still and mime their idea of a baby, singing:

> It was this way and that way,
> That way and this way,
> When I was a baby,
> Then this way went I.

They rejoin hands and walk round singing:

> When I was a lady,
> A lady, a lady,
> When I was a lady,
> How happy was I.

They stand still again and mime a lady, singing:

> It was this way and that way,
> That way and this way,
> When I was a lady,
> Then this way went I.

And so on, inventing who they should 'be' and what they should 'do' as they go round until exhausted.

First Singing Games

Children join hands and dance round in a circle three times. At the last line, they all fall down, and then, with their hands still joined, they pull each other up while they sing the second verse:

THREE times round went our gallant, gallant ship,
And three times round went she;
Three times round went our gallant, gallant ship,
Till she sank to the bottom of the sea.

Pull her up, pull her up, said the little sailor boy,
    Pull her up, pull her up, said he,
Pull her up, pull her up, said the little sailor boy,
    Or she'll sink to the bottom of the sea.

Then the children all fall down again. The game can be repeated many times.

First Singing Games

All the children except one sit, cross-legged, in a circle on the floor. The odd child walks round the outside of the circle, holding up a shoe and saying:

COBBLER, cobbler, mend my shoe,
Get it done by half-past two.
Stitch it up and stitch it down.

The circle calls:

That will cost you half a crown!

The shoe is taken into the circle and, when the 'odd-child-out' has turned his back, it is hidden under one of the crossed legs. When he returns for his shoe, it is nowhere to be found, so he runs round the outside of the circle trying to spot it. The shoe is now passed under the crossed legs of the children in the circle, and whoever has it when 'odd' manages to get hold of it, must go round with the shoe when the game is repeated.

First Singing Games

Two children join hands, and raise their arms to make an arch. The others run round and under the arch, holding on to each other's skirts or jerseys, singing the rhyme.

The two children, who are the 'arch', lower their arms and catch whoever happens to be passing under at that moment. The others withdraw, while the 'arch' tells the prisoner to choose a bird, a 'robin' or a 'thrush'. He must then go behind one of the 'arch', according to his choice.

When everyone is caught, the game ends with a tug of war between the two sides.

ALL the birdies in the air,
In the air, in the air,
All the birdies in the air,
Tickle tail to my tail!

First Singing Games

One child is chosen to be the Farmer, while the others join hands and dance round him singing:

> THERE was a farmer had a dog,
>   His name was Bobby Bingo.
> B-I-N-G-O, B-I-N-G-O, B-I-N-G-O,
>   His name was Bobby Bingo.

Here the ring stands still, while the farmer points to one player, who calls: B
>   the next, who calls: I
>   the next, who calls: N
>   the next, who calls: G
>   the next, who calls: O,
and who is now the Farmer.
Then they all sing:

> And Bingo was his name!

and the game is repeated.

The children join hands in a ring, and dance round singing the refrain: 'Here we go looby loo'. They stand still and mime the words of each alternate verse, then, joining hands, they dance round again, singing the refrain.

> HERE we go looby loo,
>   Here we go looby light,
> Here we go looby loo,
>   All on a Saturday night!

First Singing Games

Put your right foot in,
　Put your right foot out,
Shake it a little, a little,
　And turn yourself about.

Here we go looby loo, etc.

Put your left foot in,
　Put your left foot out,
Shake it a little, a little,
　And turn yourself about.

Here we go looby loo, etc.

Put your right hand in,
　Put your right hand out,
Shake it a little, a little,
　And turn yourself about.

Here we go looby loo, etc.

Put your left hand in,
　Put your left hand out,
Shake it a little, a little,
　And turn yourself about.

First Singing Games

This is a simpler version of the Looby Loo. The children join hands in a ring and dance round singing until the last word, 'Hi', when they kick up one leg and reverse the direction, repeating the game and the rhyme, until exhausted.

SALLY go round the sun,
Sally go round the moon,
Sally go round the chimney-pots
On a Sunday afternoon—Hi!

Holding the child by the waist, jump him up and down, repeating the first two lines of the rhyme. At the word 'three', the child flings his legs round your waist. Then, holding him securely, allow him to fall backwards, until his head almost touches the ground. Swing him to and fro in this position, saying: 'Under the water, catching fishes . . .'. The child is asked: 'Dead or alive?' If he answers: 'Alive', pull him up so that he can jump, feet first, to the ground again. If he says 'Dead!', let him fall on to the ground.

AMERICAN jump! American jump!
One—Two—Three!
Under the water catching fishes,
Catching fishes for my tea.
            Dead or Alive?

First Singing Games

The children sit round in a circle. Each one is given the name of a musical instrument, which he or she must imitate whenever that instrument is mentioned. All the words of the rhyme are sung in chorus, but the *sounds* in capital letters should be made by the appropriate instrument only. One child, or an adult, is chosen as the Conductor, who stands in the middle of the circle, and sees that the players come in with their instruments at the right time.

WE CAN play the Big Bass Drum,
    And this is the music to it:
RUM BOOM BOOM goes the Big Bass Drum,
    And this is the way to do it.

First Singing Games

We can play on the Bugle Horn,
    And this is the music to it:
TA TA TARAH goes the Bugle Horn,
RUM BOOM BOOM goes the Big Bass Drum,
    And this is the way to do it.

We can play on the Double Bass,
    And this is the music to it:
ZOOM ZOOM ZOOM goes the Double Bass,
TA TA TARAH goes the Bugle Horn,
RUM BOOM BOOM goes the Big Bass Drum,
    And this is the way to do it.

First Singing Games

We can play on the Tambourine,
　　And this is the music to it:
JING A TING TING goes the Tambourine,
ZOOM ZOOM ZOOM goes the Double Bass,
TA TA TARAH goes the Bugle Horn,
RUM BOOM BOOM goes the Big Bass Drum,
　　And this is the way to do it.

With each verse another instrument is added, until in the last verse *all* are included. Then it will go something like this:

We can play on the little Flute,
　　And this is the music to it:
TOOTLE TOOTLE TOOT goes the little Flute:
MEENY MINN MINN goes the Violin,
RUMA TUM TUM goes the Kettle Drum,
PLOM PLIM PLOM goes the Old Banjo,
TICKA TICKA TECK go the Castanets,
JING A TING TING goes the Tambourine,
ZOOM ZOOM ZOOM goes the Double Bass,
TA TA TARAH goes the Bugle Horn,
RUM BOOM BOOM goes the Big Bass Drum,
　　AND THIS IS THE WAY TO DO IT!

There is, of course, no limit to the number of instruments that can be added, invented and duplicated, including Vacuum Cleaners, Washing Boards, etc.

Index of First Lines

INDEX OF FIRST LINES

INDEX OF FIRST LINES